Lille

Travel Guide

2024-2025

The Complete Traveler's Companion To The Beauty Of Northern France

By

Conor Flynn

Let's Explore one of the beautiful cities in northern France.

A less talked city, but one of the perfect places in France for weekend getaway, tourism or vacation.

Let's get to LILLE ♥

Dedication

This book is a sincere commendation for your love of learning and exploring. It's designed for people who enjoy discovery and the thrill of finding hidden gems, during holidays, Vacations, business or just visiting. I hope you will experience the warmth of Lille's embrace and the fascination of its hidden beauties as you turn the pages of this book.

This dedication is extended to the kind people of Lille, whose friendliness is unending. Travelers from all over the world find Comfort here because of your generosity and charity.

This dedication is to all of the beautiful scenery, from Vieux Lille, and Palais des Beaux-Arts to the beautiful hotels, vibrant Marché, and all other attractions in this city. Your soul-stirring beauty arouses the imagination and leaves a lasting impression on everyone who sees you. This book is devoted to the spirit of adventure that beats within every one of us with boundless admiration. May it serve as a beacon of inspiration, guiding you on countless journeys filled with wonders, discovery, and unforgettable moments, with boundless gratitude and excitement

Table of Contents

How to scan the QR code in this book.

- Use your smartphone Camera
- Aim your camera at the QR code, make sure it is clearly visible within the Camera's frame.
- Hold your device steadily, and let the camera recognize the Code. It will process within a few seconds.
- Follow the prompt.

How to use the QR Code

After scanning the QR code you will be linked directly to your Google map.

Where you will now click direction.

Just put in your current Location, click start and it will start directing you to your destination.

Cheers!!!! and enjoy your stay.

Introduction

Welcome to Lille

Lille is in the heart of northern France, Lille is a vibrant city brimming with a rich history, culture, and modern beauty. Known for its beautiful architecture, bustling markets, and delectable cuisine, Lille offers an enchanting blend of Flemish and French influences. Lille promises a captivating experience for every traveler.

Lille's strategic location, close to Belgium and within easy reach of major European cities, makes it a perfect destination for short getaways and longer stays. Lille is filled with cafes and shops, serene parks, and gardens that provide a peaceful retreat. Lille is not just a destination, it is an invitation to explore, discover, and fall in love with the beauty of northern France.

How to Use This Guide

This travel guide is designed to be your comprehensive companion as you explore Lille. To help you make the most of your visit, we've organized the guide into several key sections:

Brief Overview of History: A concise look at Lille's past, from its early beginnings to its modern-day significance.

Why Visit Lille?: Highlights of what makes Lille a must-visit destination, including testimonials from other travelers.

Visa Requirements: Essential information on entry requirements and visa applications.

Accommodation Options: A detailed guide to where to stay, from luxury hotels to budget-friendly options.

Getting to Lille and Navigating Around: Tips on how to reach Lille and get around the city with ease.

Top Site Attractions, Cuisine, and Culture: Must-see landmarks, culinary delights, and cultural experiences that define Lille.

Best Time to Visit and Safety Tips: Advice on the best times to visit and important safety tips for travelers.

Practical Information: Useful details on language, currency, communication, and more to help you navigate your stay.

Just flip to the page that attracts you more and read through.

Map of Lille

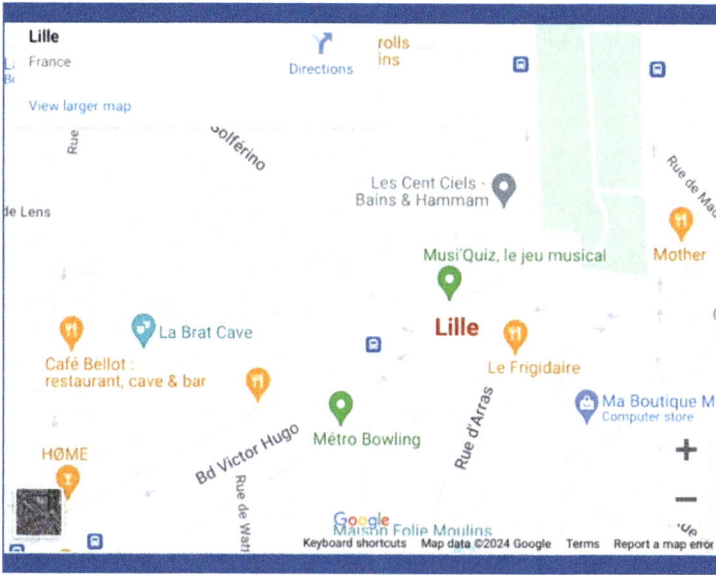

Use this map as a reference to get a sense of the city's layout and to plan your routes as you explore Lille. The map will help you locate major landmarks, navigate different neighborhoods, and discover the best spots for dining, shopping, and sightseeing.

Chapter One: Brief Overview of History

Early Beginnings

Lille's story begins in the Middle Ages, around the 7th century. Originally a small village known as L'Isle, it was built on an island in the Deûle River. The strategic location made it a natural hub for trade and commerce, drawing settlers and merchants from far and wide. By the 11th century, Lille had grown into a bustling town, surrounded by fortifications to protect its valuable market and burgeoning population.

Medieval Lille

The medieval period was a time of prosperity and growth for Lille. It became the capital of the County of Flanders, flourishing as a center of trade and culture. The cloth industry was particularly important, with weavers producing some of the finest fabrics in Europe. The town's wealth attracted the attention of various European powers, and Lille found itself at the heart of numerous conflicts and sieges. Despite these challenges, the city's resilience shone through, with each rebuilding bringing new architectural splendors and a deeper sense of community.

Industrial Revolution

The 19th century they brought the Industrial Revolution, transforming Lille into an industrial powerhouse. The city's location and existing trade networks made it a prime spot for factories and new industries. Textile production remained the primary industry, with the establishment of machinery, chemicals, and food processing sectors. This period saw rapid urbanization, with the population booming and new neighborhoods springing up to accommodate workers and their families. However, industrialization also brought social challenges, including labor disputes and harsh working conditions.

Modern Lille

Today, Lille is a dynamic city that has reinvented itself while honoring its rich history. The decline of traditional industries in the late 20th century led to significant economic challenges, the city displayed resilience and innovation in response. Extensive urban renewal projects have transformed former industrial areas into vibrant cultural and commercial hubs. The arrival of the TGV high-speed train and the Eurostar link to London has cemented Lille's status as a key European crossroads.

Modern Lille is a blend of old and new, where historic buildings stand alongside new architecture. The city is known for its lively cultural scene, prestigious educational institutions, and thriving tech and service sectors. You will feel the unique and captivating atmosphere as you walk through the street.

Why Visit Lille?

Lille is often described as a hidden gem in northern France. Its unique blend of French and Flemish influences gives the city a distinct character that's different from other French cities. Its stunning architecture and its vibrant cultural scene make Lille a rich experience. The city's compact size makes it easy to explore, and its welcoming atmosphere ensures that visitors feel right at home.

One of Lille's standout features is its food. The city is a paradise for food lovers, boasting an array of culinary delights that reflect its unique heritage. Lille's cuisine is sure to impress.

Testimonials and Quotes from Travelers

"Lille is a city that took me by surprise. The blend of French and Flemish cultures is fascinating, and the food is simply amazing!" – Sarah, USA

"I fell in love with the old town. The architecture is beautiful, and there's so much to see and do. It's a perfect weekend getaway." – Marc, Belgium

"From the museums to the markets, there's something for everyone in Lille. It's a city that truly offers a bit of everything." – Daniel, Germany

Best Time to Visit.

The temperatures are not high in the north though the best time to visit largely depends on what you're looking to experience.

I suggest you get there between April and September. Lille has fewer visitors this period. It's perfect if you want to visit Lille with fewer people. However, many bars, restaurants, and stores are closed.

But if you want a peak tourist period you should go during summer.

Summer is the busiest time of the year, with many tourists flocking to the city. Attractions, restaurants, and hotels can be crowded, and accommodation prices tend to be higher during this period.

- **Let me tell you about the different weather conditions in Lille.**

Spring (March to May): Spring in Lille is a beautiful time to visit, with mild temperatures ranging from 10°C to 18°C (50°F to 64°F). The city's parks and gardens are in full bloom, creating the perfect setting for outdoor activities and sightseeing.

Summer (June to August): "Summer is the peak tourist season.", with warm temperatures averaging 18°C to 25°C (64°F to 77°F). This is an excellent time for outdoor festivals and events, but expect larger crowds and higher accommodation prices.

Autumn (September to November): Autumn brings cooler temperatures, ranging from 8°C to 16°C (46°F to 61°F). The fall foliage adds a picturesque backdrop to the city's historic streets. It's also a great time to enjoy cultural events and festivals like La Grande Braderie de Lille.

Winter (December to February): Winter is the off-season with temperatures between 1°C and 7°C (34°F to 45°F). While it's cold, it's also the time for Lille's charming Christmas market, making it a magical period to visit. Additionally, winter sees fewer tourists, offering a quieter experience.

Chapter Two: Visa Requirements

Entry Requirements for EU and Non-EU Travelers.

EU Travelers.

If you hold a passport from a European Union country, you can visit Lille without needing a visa. Just bring your valid passport or national ID card, and you are good to go. There is no limit to how long you can stay, so you can take your time exploring all that Lille has to offer.

Non-EU Travelers.

For visitors from outside the EU, visa requirements vary depending on your country of origin. Citizens of many countries, including the USA, Canada, Australia, and Japan, can enter France for short stays (up to 90 days) without a visa. However, you will need a valid passport with at least six months of validity beyond your planned departure date.

If you're from a country that requires a visa to enter France, you'll need to apply for a Schengen visa. This visa allows you to travel within the Schengen Area, which includes most EU countries, for up to 90 days within 180 days.

How to Apply for a Visa.

- Determine Your Visa Type.

For short tourist stays, you'll need a Schengen visa. If you plan to stay longer or have specific purposes (study, work), check the specific visa category you need.

- Gather Required Documents

Completed visa application form

Valid passport (with at least two blank pages)

Recent passport-sized photos

Evidence of travel insurance with a minimum €30,000 medical emergency coverage

Verification of lodging (hotel reservations, invitation letter)

Evidence of enough financial resources, such as bank statements and a sponsorship letter

Return flight tickets or travel itinerary.

- Schedule an Appointment.

Visit the website of the French consulate or embassy in your country to schedule an appointment. Some countries may also have authorized visa application centers that handle Schengen visa applications.

- Keep Your Appointment

Carry with you the necessary paperwork, and be ready to respond to inquiries on your trip itinerary.

- Pay the Visa Fee.

The fee for a Schengen visa is typically around €80 for adults. Certain groups of travelers, such as students and children, may qualify for discounted fees.

- Wait for Processing

Visa processing times can vary, but it usually takes about 15 days. It's crucial to apply well in advance of the dates on which you want to go.

Customs Regulations and Tips

When traveling to Lille, It is important to familiarize yourself with customs regulations to ensure a smooth entry into France. Here's what you need to know:

- Duty-Free Allowances

If you're arriving from outside the EU, you can bring in certain items without paying customs duties. Here's what you're allowed to bring:

Alcohol: You can bring in 1 liter of spirits over 22% alcohol or 2 liters of fortified wine, sparkling wine, or other beverages with less than 22% alcohol. Alternatively, you can bring in 4 liters of still wine and 16 liters of beer.

Tobacco: You're allowed to bring in 200 cigarettes, 100 cigarillos, 50 cigars, or 250 grams of tobacco.

Other Goods: Personal items and gifts within reasonable quantities for personal use are generally accepted.

- Prohibited and Restricted Items

Certain items are prohibited or restricted from entering France. Be careful not to bring any of the following:

Weapons and Ammunition: Firearms and explosives are strictly controlled and require special permits.

Plants and Animal Products: Some plants, fruits, vegetables, and animal products are restricted to prevent the spread of diseases.

Counterfeit Goods: It is illegal to bring in counterfeit items or goods that infringe on intellectual property rights.

- Declaring Goods

If you're bringing in goods that exceed your duty-free allowances or if they are intended for commercial use, you must declare them at customs. Be prepared to pay customs duties on these items. Ensure you keep receipts and documentation for any items you declare.

Cash declaration: When entering or leaving France, you must declare any amount exceeding €10,000 in cash or its equivalent in other currencies. This includes physical cash, traveler's checks, bonds, and other negotiable instruments.

<u>Tips for Smooth Travel</u>

1 . Keep Receipts: Always keep receipts for high-value items and purchases. This will help if you need to declare them.

Please remember the following information:

2. Check for Restrictions: Before you travel, make sure to check if there are any specific restrictions or additional requirements for your items, especially if they are unusual or valuable.

3. Be Honest: If you're unsure about whether an item needs to be declared, it's better to declare it. Being honest with customs officials will save you time and potential fines.

4 . Consult the Website: For the most accurate and updated information, visit the official French customs website or contact the French consulate before your trip.

Chapter Three:
Accommodation Options

Luxury Hotels

Lille boasts a selection of luxury hotels that combine elegance, comfort, and exceptional service, making sure that even the most discerning traveler has a memorable stay.

Staying at one of these luxury hotels will provide a comfortable and indulgent retreat after a day of sightseeing, adding a touch of elegance to your Lille experience.

I will write about five standout luxurious hotel options, with their addresses, opening hours, and cost per night. Please note that you can search online for other luxurious hotels suitable for you.

Make sure you look at their reviews before lodging.

1 . Hôtel Barrière Lille

Location: 777 bis Pont de Flandres, 59777 Lille, France

Located near the Euralille business district, Hôtel Barrière Lille is a modern 5-star hotel known for its top-notch amenities and impeccable service.

Guests can enjoy:

- Chic, modern rooms have floor-to-ceiling windows
- Free Wi-Fi and flat-screens
- There's an upscale French restaurant and a stylish brasserie with a terrace
- Sleek sports lounge
- Hip bar with a dance floor.
- Paid parking is available.
- A luxurious spa for relaxation and rejuvenation
- Fitness center
- Currency exchange
- Pets are welcome, but please note that there is an additional charge.
- A central location close to shopping centers and major attractions,

making it an excellent base for exploring the city

Cost per Night: Starting at $220 or €202.66

Opening Hours: 24 hours

Hôtel Barrière Lille

Quick Euralille

View larger map

SKEMA Ventures

Momen'Tea Euralille

Carrefour Lille

Primark
Clothing store

Indigo - Euralille

Casino Barrière Lille

Hôtel Barrière Lille
4.5 ★ (1383)
5-star

Ferme pédagogiqu
Marcel Dhénin - Ville.

Pont de Flandres

Parc des
Dondaines

Parking Casino
Barrière Lille-Fives

Av. Willy Br

Google

Keyboard shortcuts   Map data ©2024 Google   Terms   Report a map error

How To Scan The QR Code

- Ensure your smartphone has a camera.
- Open the Camera App,you don't need any special settings the regular photo mode will often work.
- Aim your camera at the QR code. Make sure the QR code is clearly visible within the camera's frame.
- Hold your device steady while the camera focuses on the QR code. most camera apps will recognize the QR code automatically and process it within a few seconds.
- Follow the Prompt

2 . L'Hermitage Gantois, Autograph Collection

Located at 224 Rue Pierre Mauroy, 59000 Lille, France

This hotel is located just 4 minutes from Mairie de Lille metro station, 6 minutes away from Le Palais Des Beaux Arts de Lille, and a 15-minute walk from Gare de

Guest can enjoy:

- A serene courtyard perfect for relaxation
- A paid spa features treatments
- An indoor pool and a steam room.
- Parking and breakfast come with extra charges.
- Free Wi-Fi.
- Pets are welcome, but please note that there is an additional charge.
- No fitness center

Cost per Night: Starting at $230 or €211.85

Opening Hours: 24 hours

3 . Clarance Hotel Lille

Location of this hotel is at 32 Rue de la Barre, 59800 Lille, France.

Housed in a beautifully restored 18th-century mansion, this opulent hotel in the city center is 15-minute walk from art exhibits at the Palais des Beaux-Arts and 2 km from Lille Europe train station.

Guests can enjoy:

- Uniquely decorated rooms, each blending antique and modern furnishings
- Free Wi-Fi, TVs, minibars, and tea and coffeemakers.
- Upgraded rooms have chandeliers. Suites add living areas, and one has a 4-poster bed.
- Room service is available 24 hours.
- Paid breakfast, paid parking
- A beautiful garden and courtyard for a tranquil retreat
- No fitness center.
- No pets allowed.

Cost per Night: Starting at $200 approximately €184.23
Opening Hours: 24 hours

4 . Couvent des Minimes - Alliance Lille

This hotel is Located at 17 Quai du Wault, 59800 Lille, France

This Modern hotel is just an 8-minute walk from the Citadelle de Lille.

Guest can enjoy:

- Warm, spacious, and modern rooms
- Free Wi-Fi, flat-screen TVs and minibars,
- Meeting space and a breakfast buffet are available.
- A glass-roofed courtyard that serves as a bar and restaurant area, providing a stunning and unique dining experience
- A tranquil setting with lush gardens
- Pets are welcome, but there are additional charges.
- No fitness center
- No spa

- A peaceful atmosphere ideal for relaxation

Cost per Night: Starting at $180 or €165.81
Opening Hours: 24 hours

5 . Best Western Premier Why Hotel

Address: 7 Bis Square Morisson, 59800 Lille, France

This is a travelers' Choice, Perfectly located in the heart of Lille, this newly opened contemporary design hotel offers en suite comfortable accommodation

Guest can enjoy:
- Free Wi-Fi and a 24-hour reception.
- All the hotel rooms feature sophisticated original decor and wooden floors, equipped with a desk, and a flat-screen TV with cable channels.
- A minibar and a Nespresso
- Coffee machines are also provided for your convenience.

- Every morning, a breakfast buffet is provided in the cozy comfort of your room or the shared lounge.
- In addition, visitors may have lunch in the hotel's restaurant or unwind with a refreshing drink at the lovely bar.
- Parking is available at cost.
- The hotel has a fully equipped boardroom, available for meetings and receptions.
- A fitness center for staying active during your trip

Cost per Night: Starting at $170 or €156.58
Opening Hours: 24 hours

Boutique Hotels

Lille is home to several charming boutique hotels that offer personalized service, unique décor, and an intimate atmosphere. Here are four standout options:

1. Hotel Kanaï

Address: 10 Rue de Béthune, 59000 Lille, France

This hotel is located on a busy street in the city center and is only a 2-minute walk from the Rihour metro station, a 4-minute walk from Grand Place Square, and from the Palais des Beaux-Arts de Lille museum it is a 7-minute walk.

- The rooms, upstairs, have bright furnishings and rich color decorations.
- All have free Wi-Fi, flat-screen TVs with satellite channels, Nespresso coffee makers, and high-end toiletries.
- The suites also have living rooms with pull-out sofas.

- Room service is available around the clock, and breakfast is available for a fee
- There's no fitness center
- No spa
- No pets are allowed.

Opening Hours: 24 hours

Cost per Night: Starting at €90 or $97.71

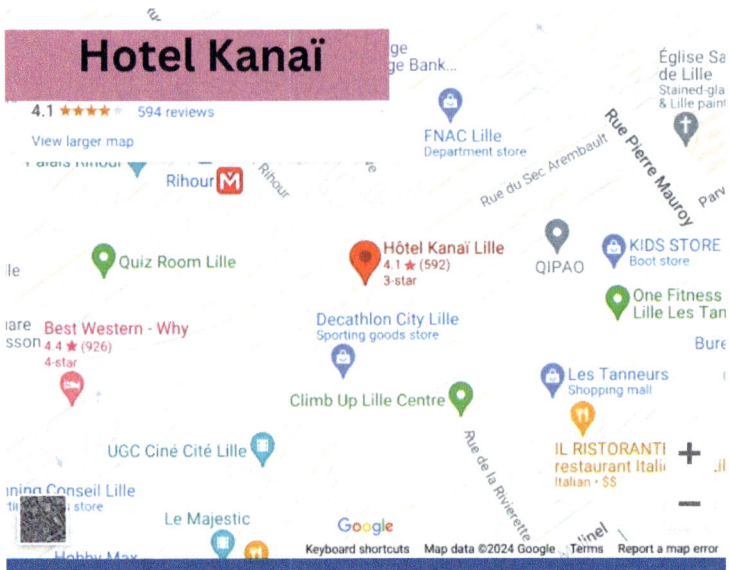

Hotel Kanaï

4.1 ★★★★☆ 594 reviews

View larger map

How To Scan The QR Code

- Ensure your smartphone has a camera.
- Open the Camera App,you don't need any special settings the regular photo mode will often work.
- Aim your camera at the QR code. Make sure the QR code is clearly visible within the camera's frame.
- Hold your device steady while the camera focuses on the QR code. most camera apps will recognize the QR code automatically and process it within a few seconds.
- Follow the Prompt

2. Mama Shelter Lille

Address:97 Pl. Saint-Hubert, 59800 Lille, France

Mama Shelter Lille is ideally situated for easy city exploration. It is only a short distance from both of Lille's main rail stations and the Euralille business district. Jalil Amor has thoughtfully created each of Mama Lille's 112 rooms to provide the perfect balance of comfort and modernity, creating a comfortable haven. The restaurant and bar welcome you at any time of the evening, whether it's to dance, enjoy a great meal, or sip a beverage.

- No fitness center
- No spa
- Pets are allowed at no charge. Both dogs and cats are permitted.

Opening Hours: 24 hours

Cost per Night: Starting at €120 or $130.28

3. L'Esplanade Lille

Address: 42b Façade de l'Esplanade, 59800 Lille, France

Situated in Lille's historic center, L'Esplanade Lille provides heated, soundproofed rooms and studios along with free Wi-Fi in common spaces. It is located 1.3 kilometers from Lille Grand Place and 1 km from Lille Citadel.

- Every room includes a flat-screen TV and a private bathroom furnished with complimentary amenities such as a bathrobe and a hair dryer.
- Guests can enjoy reading a newspaper in their room or the lounge while having the continental breakfast.
- Please note that there are no fitness centers or spa facilities on-site, and the property is pet-friendly.

Opening Hours: 24 hours

Cost per Night: Starting at €130 or $141.13

4. La Maison du Champlain

Address: 13 Rue Nicolas Leblanc, 59000 Lille, France

It's a "home away from home" here. La Maison du Champlain wants you to have the most pleasurable and restful stay possible. Beffroi de l'Hôtel and La Gare Saint Sauveur are two nearby sites that make La Maison du Champlain a fantastic spot to stay when visiting Lille.

- Among the amenities offered by this inn is a coffee shop.
- Additionally, there is a hot tub and breakfast available, which will enhance your trip to Lille.
- The street has parking available and accessible for anyone arriving at La Maison du Champlain by car.
- Popular attractions to visit include Grand Place, Palais des Beaux-Arts, and Vieux-Lille, all within walking distance from the hotel.
- There is no fitness center.
- Pets are not permitted.

Opening Hours: 24 hours
Cost per Night: Starting at €150 or $162.85

Budget Stays and Hostels

Lille offers a variety of budget accommodations and hostels that provide comfort, convenience, and a friendly atmosphere without breaking the bank. Here are five great options:

1. Gastama - The People Hostel

Address: 109 rue saint-andré, Lille City Center, Lille, Nord-Pas-de-Calais, France, 69000

Located in Lille's most picturesque neighborhood, Gastama offers a diverse range of lodging options to cater to every preference. The hostel provides opportunities for socializing and meeting people from around the world, whether guests choose to stay in private rooms or dorms. Conveniently situated in the city's historic district, Gastama is just a ten-minute walk from Lille's central plaza and twenty minutes from the rail terminals. Guests can enjoy

- A lively bar
- A shared kitchen
- Free Wi-Fi

Cost per Night: Starting at $25 (€23.03) for a dorm bed, $70(€64.49). for a private room

Opening Hours: 24 hours

2. Lille City Hotel

Address: 5 Rue de la Clef, 59800 Lille, France.

This cozy hotel is situated on a street lined with boutique shops. It's just a 3-minute walk from a metro stop, an 11-minute walk from Lille Cathedral, and a 5-minute walk from the Museum of Fine Arts.

- The simply furnished rooms are equipped with air conditioning, flat-screen TVs, en suite bathrooms, and Wi-Fi access.

- A breakfast buffet is available for an additional fee, and there's a terrace.
- No fitness center
- No spa
- Pet-friendly: Dogs and Cats allowed at extra charge
- The hotel provides a continental breakfast and has a 24-hour reception.

Cost per Night: Starting at $50(€46.06).

Opening Hours: 24 hours

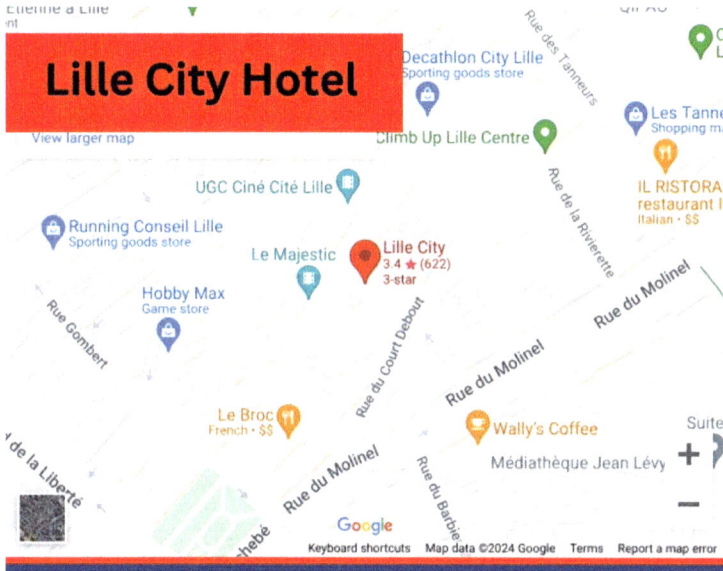

Lille City Hotel

View larger map

Etienne a Lille
Decathlon City Lille
Sporting goods store

Rue des Tanneurs

Les Tanne
Shopping ma

Climb Up Lille Centre

IL RISTORA
restaurant I
italian · $$

Rue de la Rivierette

UGC Ciné Cité Lille

Running Conseil Lille
Sporting goods store

Le Majestic

Lille City
3.4 ★ (622)
3-star

Rue du Molinel

Hobby Max
Game store

Rue Gombert

Rue du Court Debout

Rue du Molinel

Le Broc
French · $$

Wally's Coffee

Suite

de la Liberté

Rue du Molinel

Rue du Barbie

Médiathèque Jean Lévy

Google

Keyboard shortcuts   Map data ©2024 Google   Terms   Report a map error

How To Scan The QR Code

- Ensure your smartphone has a camera.
- Open the Camera App,you don't need any special settings the regular photo mode will often work.
- Aim your camera at the QR code. Make sure the QR code is clearly visible within the camera's frame.
- Hold your device steady while the camera focuses on the QR code. most camera apps will recognize the QR code automatically and process it within a few seconds.
- Follow the Prompt

48

3. Hotel Flandre Angleterre

Adresse: 13 Pl. de la Gare, 59000 Lille, France

In the heart of Lille, the cozy Hotel Flandre Angleterre is situated in a prominent area. The hotel is conveniently located near several local tourist destinations, such as the Opera, Musee des Cannoniers, and Gare Lille Flandres. Additionally, La Vieille Bourse, City Centre Lille, and Grand Place de Lille are all within proximity.

- The Hotel Flandre Angleterre does not allow smoking.
- There is a restaurant within the hotel's dining areas.
- There is a fee associated with breakfast.
- The hotel has a front desk staffed 24 hours.
- Tennis courts are among the hotel's other features.
- Additional services include free newspapers in the lobby.

- A front desk safe deposit box, and an elevator or lift.

Cost per Night: Starting at $60(€55.27).

Opening Hours: 24 hours

4. Auberge de Jeunesse HI Lille

Address: Avenue du Président Kennedy, 59000 Lille, France

Part of the Hostelling International network, this youth hostel offers dormitory beds and private rooms. It features a communal kitchen, a dining area, free Wi-Fi, and a lounge with games and books.

Cost per Night: Starting at $20 (€18.42) for a dorm bed, $50 (€46.06) for a private room

Opening Hours: 24 hours

5. Calm Appart' & Hostel

2 Rue des Buisses, 59800 Lille, France

This modern apartment hostel offers a combination of dormitory beds, private rooms, and self-catering apartments. The hotel is conveniently located just a 2-minute walk from the Gare de

Lille-Flandres rail and metro station and a 10-minute walk from Vieux-Lille.

- The airy, modern studio apartments come equipped with free Wi-Fi, flat-screen TVs, dining rooms, a shared kitchen, and a communal lounge.
- For a price, groceries may be delivered to the units.
- There's a conference room as well.
- No fitness center
- No spa
- No pets are allowed

Cost per Night: Starting at $30 (€27.63). for a dorm bed, $70 (€64.49). for a private room

Opening Hours: 24 hours

Unique Accommodation (B&Bs, Airbnb)

Lille offers a variety of unique accommodations, including lovely B&Bs

and stylish Airbnb properties, each providing a distinct experience for travelers. Here are four standout options:

1. La Villa 30

24 Rue du Plat, 59800 Lille, France

With its five rooms, La Villa 30 Guest House is in Lille Downtown. It's a property from the 1930s that has been updated with modern furnishings. Every room is inspired by Lille's top attractions and includes a private bathroom.

La Villa 30 is close to the city center. Buses, subways, and stores are all nearby.

It is located 50 meters away from the Palais des Beaux-Arts, a 7-minute walk from the railway station, a 15-minute walk from Zenith / Grand Palais, and a 15-minute drive from the airport.

- There is no fitness center, no spa
- Breakfast is free
- No parking
- Airport shuttle comes with an extra charge
- Pets are not allowed

2. Au Coeur de Lille

Address: 1 Rue Boileux, 59000 Lille, France.

Au Coeur De Lille Bed & Breakfast is located 0.8 kilometers from Place Charles de Gaulle and offers free WiFi. On-site private parking is offered for EUR 15 per day.

This B&B is located ten minutes walk from Lille's center.

For guests' convenience, the rooms have a

- flat-screen TV with satellite channels and coffee/tea-making supplies. Glassware and tea/coffee-making supplies are included.
- In addition to standard amenities like guest toiletries, there's a walk-in shower and a bath.
- The Au Coeur De Lille Bed & Breakfast serves a continental breakfast.

Cost per Night: Starting at $110 or (€101.34).

Opening Hours: 24 hours

3. Le Clos Notre Dame

Address: 11 Pl. Gilleson, 59800 Lille, France

Situated in the historic Vieux Lille district, this charming B&B offers three beautifully decorated rooms with a mix of vintage and modern décor. Guests can relax in the private courtyard garden or enjoy a homemade breakfast featuring local specialties. The friendly hosts provide a warm and inviting atmosphere.

- There is Free Wi-Fi
- No pets
- Child-friendly environment
- No fitness center
- No spa

Cost per Night: Starting at $100 or €92.13.

Opening Hours: 24 hours

4. Les Toquées Maison d'hôtes

Address: 110 Quai Géry Legrand 59000 - Lille

Les Toquées Maison d'hôtes offers free WiFi all across the property and it is situated800 meters from Zoo Park of Lille and 10 minutes by car from Nouveau Siècle Convention Centre. On-site private parking is free of charge. Some apartments include a comfortable seating space. Every room has its bathroom. Every morning there is a continental breakfast offered. The facility offers dry cleaning services. You can do a lot of other things, including kayaking and cycling. The guest home also rents out bicycles. At a distance of 9 kilometers, Lille Airport is the closest airport to the property.

Cost per Night: Starting at $170 or (€138.97).

Opening Hours: 24 hours

Tips for Booking Good Accommodation in Lille.

Booking the right accommodation can greatly enhance your experience in Lille.

Tips to help you find the perfect place to stay:

1. Determine Your Priorities

Location: Decide if you want to stay in the heart of the city near major attractions, or in a quieter neighborhood. Vieux Lille is great for historical charm, while Euralille offers modern conveniences.

Budget: Set a budget within your price range. Lille offers a variety of accommodations from budget hostels to luxury hotels and charming B&Bs.

Amenities: Consider what amenities are important to you, such as free Wi-Fi, breakfast, parking, or a gym.

2. Read Reviews

Check Multiple Sources: Read reviews on multiple platforms like TripAdvisor, Booking.com, and Airbnb to get a comprehensive view of the property.

Look for Consistency: Please take note of any recurring comments regarding cleanliness, service, and location.

Consider Recent Reviews: Make sure to prioritize recent reviews to ensure that the information is current.

3. Book Early

Peak Seasons: If you are traveling during a busy period, such as summer or Christmas markets, it is advisable to book well in advance to secure the best deals and availability.

Special Events: Be mindful of local events that could impact availability and prices, such as the Lille Braderie or music festivals.

4. Use Reputable Booking Sites

Trusted Platforms: Use well-known booking platforms like Booking.com, Expedia, or the official websites of hotels and hostels to ensure security and reliability.

Cancellation Policies: Check the cancellation policies before booking. Flexible booking options can be helpful in case your plans change.

5. Contact the Accommodation Directly

Questions and Requests: If you have specific needs or questions, contact the accommodation directly. This can also be a good way to gauge their customer service.

Special Deals: Sometimes booking directly with the hotel or B&B can result in special deals or added perks.

6. Consider Alternative Accommodations

Airbnb and HomeAway: These platforms offer unique stays and often have more flexible options for larger groups or longer stays.

B&Bs and Guesthouses: For a more personalized experience, consider staying at a bed and breakfast or guesthouse.

7. Check for Transportation Links

Public Transport: Ensure that your accommodation is conveniently located near public transportation options such as metro, bus, or train stations.

Parking: If you're driving, check if the accommodation provides parking or if there are nearby parking facilities.

8. Pay Attention to the Fine Print

Additional Fees: Look out for additional fees such as city taxes, cleaning fees, or charges for extra amenities.

House Rules: Make sure to read the house rules, especially if you're staying in a B&B or Airbnb, to avoid any surprises.

9. Safety and Security

Safe Neighborhoods: Make sure to research the safety of the neighborhood where you'll be staying.

Security Features: Check if the accommodation offers security features like a safe, 24-hour reception, or secure access.

By keeping these tips in mind, you can find the perfect accommodation in Lille that meets your needs and enhances your travel experience.

Chapter Four: Getting to Lille and Navigating Around

(a): By Air: Airports and Flights

Lille is well-connected by air, making it easily accessible from various international and domestic destinations.

The primary airport serving Lille is Lille Lesquin Airport, located approximately 11 kilometers southeast of the city center. Despite being smaller in size compared to Paris or Brussels, it accommodates a variety of flights, including domestic and European destinations.

Major airlines operating here include Air France, Ryanair, Volotea, and easyJet, offering flights to and from cities such as Paris, Lyon, Marseille, Bordeaux, and seasonal destinations like Malaga and Palma de Mallorca.

The airport offers essential facilities including car rental services, a business center, restaurants, shops, and free Wi-Fi. There's also a shuttle bus service that runs regularly between the airport and Lille city center, making the 20-minute journey convenient and hassle-free.

<u>Other Nearby Airports</u>

1 . Charles de Gaulle Airport (CDG)

Located approximately 200 kilometers from Lille, Charles de Gaulle Airport in Paris is one of Europe's busiest airports and offers extensive international and domestic flight options.

From CDG, you can take a direct TGV (high-speed train) to Lille, which takes about an hour. The TGV station is located within the airport, making the transfer straightforward.

2 . Brussels Airport (BRU)

Approximately 120 kilometers from Lille, Brussels Airport offers another alternative for international travelers. Flights all over the world can Land and take off from here. From Brussels Airport, take a train to Brussels Midi station and then a direct train to Lille. The total journey takes around 1 to 2 hours.

(b): By Train: Eurostar, TGV, and Local Trains

Traveling to Lille by train is a convenient and efficient option, because of its excellent connections with major cities in France, Belgium, and beyond. Here is an overview of the key train services you can use to reach Lille and navigate around the city.

Eurostar

The Eurostar high-speed train connects Lille with several major cities, including London, Brussels, and Paris. This is an excellent option for international travelers looking to arrive swiftly and comfortably.

Eurostar trains from London's St Pancras International Station arrive at Lille Europe station in about 1 hour and 20 minutes. Trains from Brussels Midi take around 35 minutes, while Paris Gare du Nord is approximately a 1-hour journey.

Facilities: Eurostar trains offer comfortable seating, Wi-Fi, power outlets, and a range of refreshments. It's advisable to book tickets in advance, especially during peak travel periods.

Cost:

London to Lille: Starting at approximately $100 or €92.13 one-way, depending on the time of booking and travel class.

Brussels to Lille: Starting at approximately $30 or €27.64 one-way.

Paris to Lille: Starting at approximately $40 one-way.

TGV (Train à Grande Vitesse)

The TGV is France's high-speed train service that connects Lille with other major

French cities. It's a fast and convenient way to travel within France.

TGV trains from Paris Gare du Nord to Lille Europe take about 1 hour. Other routes include connections to cities like Lyon, Marseille, and Bordeaux, with travel times varying depending on the destination.

Facilities: TGV trains are equipped with comfortable seating, WiFi, power outlets, and a dining car. If you want to secure the best fare, booking in advance is recommended.

Cost:

Paris to Lille: From $50 (€46.06) one-way.

Lyon to Lille: From $120 (€110.58) one-way.

Marseille to Lille: From $150 (€138.18) one-way.

Local Trains

Local trains, operated by SNCF and TER (Transport Express Régional), connect Lille with nearby towns and cities within the Hauts-de-France region and beyond.

Routes and Travel Times: Local trains from Lille Flandres station connect to cities such as Roubaix, Tourcoing, and Arras. For example, a train to Roubaix takes around 20 minutes, while Tourcoing is about 30 minutes away.

Facilities: Local trains are generally comfortable and offer basic amenities. They are a practical option for shorter journeys within the region.

Cost:

Lille to Roubaix: from $10 (€9.21) one-way.

Lille to Arras: from $15 (€13.82) one-way.

Booking and Tickets

Booking: Tickets for Eurostar, TGV, and local trains can be purchased online via the respective train operators' websites, at the train stations, or through third-party booking platforms.

Advance Purchase: For Eurostar and TGV services, booking in advance is highly recommended to secure the best fares and ensure availability.

Passes: Consider purchasing a rail pass if you plan to travel extensively by train within France or Europe.

c): By Road: Driving and Car Rentals

Driving to Lille provides flexibility and the chance to explore the surrounding regions at your own pace. Here's what you need to know about driving and renting a car for your trip to Lille.

From Paris: Lille is approximately 220 kilometers north of Paris, which translates to about a 2-hour drive via the A1 motorway. The route is straightforward and well-signposted.

From Brussels: Lille is around 120 kilometers southwest of Brussels, with a driving time of about 1 hour via the A27 and A1 motorways.

From London: The drive from London to Lille takes about 3 hours, covering approximately 250 kilometers. You'll need to cross the English Channel via the

Eurotunnel or take a ferry to Calais and then continue by road.

Cost of Driving:

Fuel: The cost of fuel will vary based on your vehicle and current fuel prices. For example, a drive from Paris to Lille would require roughly 20-25 liters of fuel, costing around $30 (€27.64)-$40 (€36.85) based on average fuel prices.

Toll Costs: Motorways in France often have tolls. For a journey from Paris to Lille, expect to pay around $15 (€13.82)-$20(€18.43) in tolls.

Eurotunnel: If driving from London, the Eurotunnel crossing costs approximately $150(€138.18)-$200 (€184.23) for a round trip with a standard car, depending on the time of booking and vehicle size.

Car Rentals in Lille

Lille has several car rental agencies, including major brands like Hertz, Avis, Enterprise, and Europcar. These can be found at Lille Lesquin Airport, Lille Europe train station, and various city locations.

The prices of renting a car vary based on the type of vehicle, the duration you will be renting, and rental company. On average, expect to pay:

Economy Car: Prices start at approximately $40 (€36.85) to $60 (€55.27) per day.

Standard Car: Prices start at approximately $60 (€55.27) to $90 (€82.89) per day.

Luxury Car: Prices start at approximately $100 (€92.13) to $150 (€138.18) per day.

Additional Costs: Don't forget about possible extra expenses like insurance, GPS rental, and fuel. Some rental companies may also charge a one-way fee if you plan to drop off the car at a different location.

Parking in Lille

City Center: Parking in the city center can be challenging and may require paying for parking at metered spots or in public parking garages. Rates typically range from $2 (€1.84) to $5 (€4.64) per hour.

Public Parking: Several public parking facilities are available, such as the Euralille shopping center parking and the Gare Lille Europe parking. These offer both short-term and long-term parking options.

Parking Apps: Use parking apps or websites to find and reserve parking spots in advance, which can be particularly useful during busy periods.

Driving and renting a car provides flexibility and convenience, allowing you to explore Lille and its surroundings at your own pace. Be sure to plan your route, check parking options, and consider the costs involved to ensure a smooth and enjoyable trip.

(d): Public Transport: Buses, Metro, and Trams

Lille boasts of an efficient and user-friendly public transport system, making it easy to navigate the city and its surroundings.

Metro

Lille's metro system consists of two lines that cover the city and extend into neighboring areas. Line 1 runs from the south of the city to the north, while Line 2 connects the east to the west. The metro is a quick and reliable way to get around.

Cost:

Single Ticket: Approximately $2.50 (€2.30). This ticket allows one journey within the metro system and includes connections to buses and trams within 1 hour.

Day Pass: Approximately $6.00 (€5.53). Valid for unlimited travel on the metro, buses, and trams for one day.

Opening Hours: The metro operates from around 5:00 AM to 12:30 AM, with extended hours on weekends.

Buses

The bus network in Lille is extensive, covering routes throughout the city and extending to surrounding suburbs. Buses are a good option for reaching areas not served by the metro or tram.

Cost:

Single Ticket: Approximately $2.50 (€2.30). Valid for one journey on the bus and includes connections to the metro and trams within 1 hour.

Day Pass: Approximately $6.00 (€5.53). Offers unlimited travel on buses, the metro, and trams for one day.

Opening Hours: Buses generally run from around 6:00 AM to 8:00 PM. Some routes may offer extended services during peak hours.

Trams

Lille's tram system consists of two lines that connect the city center with surrounding towns and suburbs. The tram is a scenic way to travel and offers a pleasant experience for longer journeys.

Cost:

Single Ticket: Approximately $2.50 (€2.30). This ticket is valid for one tram ride and includes connections to the metro and buses within 1 hour.

Day Pass: Approximately $6.00 (€5.53). Provides unlimited travel on trams, the metro, and buses for one day.

Opening Hours: Trams operate from around 5:00 AM to 12:30 AM, with some lines offering extended services on weekends.

Tickets and Passes

Purchase Locations: Tickets and passes can be bought at metro and tram stations, from ticket vending machines, or through the Transpole app. The app also offers the convenience of purchasing and storing digital tickets.

Transfers: Tickets for the metro, buses, and trams are interchangeable, allowing you to transfer between different modes of transport within the 1-hour validity period.

<u>Tips for Using Public Transport in Lille</u>

Check Timetables: Timetables and frequency of services can vary, so it's a good idea to check schedules in advance, especially if traveling early in the morning or late at night.

Validate Your Ticket: Ensure you validate your ticket before boarding. Validation machines are located at metro entrances and on trams and buses.

Peak Hours: Be aware of peak hours (typically 7:30 AM to 9:00 AM and 5:00 PM to 7:00 PM) when public transport can be crowded.

(e): Biking

Lille's compact and picturesque layout makes it an ideal city for both biking and walking. Here's how you can make the most of exploring Lille on two wheels or by foot.

Biking

Lille is equipped with dedicated bike lanes and paths, especially in the city center and along major routes. These lanes are well-marked and generally safe for cyclists. Popular cycling routes include paths along the Deûle River and through the scenic areas of Vieux Lille. The city's flat terrain makes biking easy and enjoyable.

Lille offers a bike-sharing service called V'Lille, with numerous stations scattered throughout the city. It's a convenient option for both short trips and longer rides.

Cost:

Single Ride: Approximately $1.50(€1.38). for the first 30 minutes. After that, additional charges apply, typically around $0.50 for each additional 30 minutes.

Day Pass: Approximately $5.00(€4.61). for unlimited rides within 24 hours.

How to Use: You can rent a bike by purchasing a ticket at V'Lille stations or through the V'Lille app. The app also allows you to locate available bikes and docking stations.

Bike Rentals

Local Shops: Various local bike rental shops offer a range of bicycles, including city bikes, electric bikes, and mountain bikes. Rental prices typically start at around $15-$20 (€13.82 - €18.42) Per day.

Renting from a local shop can provide you with maps and local advice on the best routes and attractions.

(f): Walking

Lille's city center, especially the historic area of Vieux Lille, is ideal for walking. Its narrow streets, charming squares, and historic buildings are best explored on foot. Stroll through the Grand Place to admire its stunning architecture, explore the streets of

Vieux Lille, or wander through the picturesque Parc Barbieux.

Consider joining a walking tour to learn more about Lille's history and architecture. Many tours are available, covering various themes such as historical landmarks, culinary experiences, or art and culture.

 Maps and guides are available at tourist information centers, providing routes to major attractions and hidden gems.

Safety and Tips

Be aware of pedestrian-only zones in the city center, where vehicles are restricted. These areas are perfect for leisurely walks and enjoying local cafes and shops.

Check the weather before setting out, as Lille can be rainy. Dress appropriately and carry an umbrella if needed.

Comfortable walking shoes are recommended, especially if you plan to explore the city extensively.

(g): Taxis and Ride-Sharing

Taxis are readily available, especially at major transport hubs and popular spots.

Ride-sharing: Services like Uber operate in Lille, providing a convenient and often more affordable alternative to traditional taxis.

With a variety of transportation options, getting to Lille and navigating around the city is straightforward, allowing you to focus on enjoying all that this vibrant city has to offer.

Chapter Five: Top Site Attractions, Cuisine, and Culture.

Where to visit in Lille (Historical Landmarks)

- ### Palais des Beaux-Arts

Located in the heart of Lille, the Palais des Beaux-Arts is one of the most prominent museums in France, second only to the Louvre in Paris in terms of the richness of its collections. This stunning building, built in the late 19th century, houses an extensive collection of European paintings, sculptures, and antiquities. Notable works include pieces by Rubens, Goya, and Delacroix, as well as a remarkable collection of 17th- and 18th-century ceramics.

Location: Place de la République, 59000 Lille, France.

Opening Hours:

Monday: Closed

Tuesday to Sunday: 10:00 AM - 6:00 PM

First Sunday of each month: Free entry

Cost of Entrance:

General Entrance: €7 (approximately $8)

Reduced Entrance: €4 (approximately $4.50) for students, seniors, and groups

Free for children under 12 and for everyone on the first Sunday of the month.

Palais des Beaux-Arts

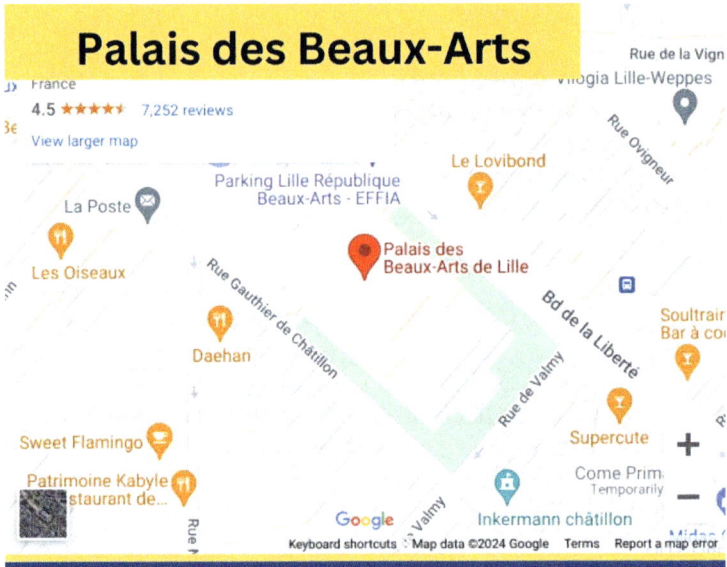

France

4.5 ★★★★★ 7,252 reviews

View larger map

Palais des Beaux-Arts de Lille

Rue de la Vign

Vilogia Lille-Weppes

Rue Ovigneur

Le Lovibond

Parking Lille République
Beaux-Arts - EFFIA

La Poste

Les Oiseaux

Rue Gauthier de Châtillon

Daehan

Bd de la Liberté

Rue de Valmy

Soultrair
Bar à co

Sweet Flamingo

Patrimoine Kabyle
staurant de...

Supercute

Come Prim
Temporarily

Inkermann châtillon

Google

Keyboard shortcuts   Map data ©2024 Google   Terms   Report a map error

How To Scan The QR Code

- Ensure your smartphone has a camera.
- Open the Camera App,you don't need any special settings the regular photo mode will often work.
- Aim your camera at the QR code. Make sure the QR code is clearly visible within the camera's frame.
- Hold your device steady while the camera focuses on the QR code. most camera apps will recognize the QR code automatically and process it within a few seconds.
- Follow the Prompt

81

- Vieille Bourse

The Vieille Bourse, or Old Stock Exchange, is one of Lille's most iconic and beautiful buildings. Constructed between 1652 and 1653, this stunning example of Flemish Renaissance architecture is an assembly of 24 identical small houses forming a square-shaped courtyard.

The courtyard is a lively space where you can find second-hand booksellers, chess players, and occasional flower markets. The Vieille Bourse often hosts cultural events, such as concerts, dance performances, and art exhibitions.

Cost for Entry:

The courtyard and book market are open to the public, allowing you to experience the atmosphere without any cost. But Some special events or exhibitions hosted at the Vieille Bourse might have an entrance fee. Prices depend on the event.

Opening Hours:

From Monday to Saturday: 1:00 PM - 7:00 PM

Closed on Sundays and public holidays.
Address: Place du Général de Gaulle, 59000
Lille, France

- Vieux Lille (Old Town)

Both locals and visitors adore the Vieux
Lille, which is a great place for a stroll or a
shopping excursion. The Vieux Lille hasn't
changed since the 18th century and has
withstood the wars. You will stroll and
admire the Flemish architecture, and have
a drink at a café. There are various
bakeries, breweries, and restaurants.

THE TOWN HALL'S BELFRY

The biggest belfry in Europe, the Lille belfry
is a UNESCO World Heritage site! 104
meters (341 feet) high and opened in 1932,
it offers a 360-degree panorama of Lille.
You'll need to utilize an elevator after
ascending 109 stairs to see the view.
Alternatively, you can continue walking up
the 300 steps. Although admission costs
7.50 euros, the first Wednesday of each
month is free. For an additional two euros,

you may get an audio guide. It will describe the belfry's past.

- Lille Citadel

Lille is a city with green spaces! With a total area of 110 hectares, Citadelle Park is a popular place among locals.

The Lille Citadel, also known as the "Queen of Citadels," is a remarkable example of 17th-century military architecture. Designed by the famed French military engineer Sébastien Le Prestre de Vauban to protect Lille, this star-shaped fortress is one of the best-preserved of its kind. It is beautifully surrounded by parkland that stretches all around the citadel. You will find a canal, a zoo, and a merry-go-round and you can go on a treetop adventure course there.

Cost for Entry:

Entry to the exterior grounds and Parc de la Citadelle is free.

Guided tours of the interior are occasionally available but must be arranged in advance, as the citadel is an active military site. The cost for these tours, when available, can vary. It's best to check with the Lille tourist office for current pricing and availability.

Opening Hours:

The exterior grounds and Parc de la Citadelle are open daily from 8:00 AM to 8:00 PM.

Access to the interior is restricted, so if you're interested in a tour, contact the local tourist office for details.

Located at Avenue du 43e Régiment d'Infanterie, 59800 Lille, France

- LaM - Lille Métropole Musée d'art Moderne, d'Art Contemporain et d'Art Brut

Located in Villeneuve-d'Ascq, just outside Lille, LaM is a museum dedicated to modern, contemporary, and outsider art. Its collection includes works by Picasso, Modigliani, and Miró, as well as a significant collection of art brut (outsider art).

Located at 1 Allée du Musée, 59650 Villeneuve-d'Ascq, France

Opening Hours:

Monday: Closed

Tuesday to Sunday: 10:00 AM - 6:00 PM

Cost of Entrance:

General Admission: €10 (approximately $11)

Reduced Admission: €7 (approximately $8) for students, seniors, and groups

Free for children under 12 and for everyone on the first Sunday of the month

- Musée de l'Hospice Comtesse

Housed in a former hospice founded in the 13th century, this museum offers a fascinating glimpse into Lille's history and heritage. The collection includes medieval and Renaissance art, as well as artifacts related to the city's past.

Located at 32 Rue de la Monnaie, 59800 Lille, France

Opening Hours:

Monday: Closed

Tuesday to Sunday: 10:00 AM - 6:00 PM

Cost of Entrance:

General Admission: €3.70 (approximately $4)

Reduced Admission: €2.60 (approximately $3) for students, seniors, and groups

Free for children under 12 and for everyone on the first Sunday of the month.

- Musée d'Histoire Naturelle de Lille

The Natural History Museum of Lille is perfect for families and anyone interested in the natural world. The museum features extensive collections in zoology, geology, and paleontology, with engaging exhibits that educate and entertain.

Location: 19 Rue de Bruxelles, 59000 Lille, France

Opening Hours:

Monday: Closed

Tuesday to Friday: 9:30 AM - 5:00 PM

Saturday and Sunday: 10:00 AM - 6:00 PM

Cost of Entrance:

General Admission: €4 (approximately $4.50)

Reduced Admission: €2.60 (approximately $3) for students, seniors, and groups

Free for children under 12 and for everyone on the first Sunday of the month

- **La Piscine - Musée d'Art et d'Industrie**

Located at 23 Rue de l'Espérance, 59100 Roubaix, France

It's not in Lille but in Roubaix which is not far! Piscine means swimming pool. It's called Piscine Museum because it used to be a swimming pool in the past

La Piscine offers a unique setting for its diverse collection, which includes fine arts, applied arts, and industrial heritage.

You'll find their paintings, sculptures but also fabrics, graphic art, or photography.

Opening Hours:

Monday: Closed

From Tuesday to Thursday: 11:00 AM - 6:00 PM

Friday: 11:00 AM - 8:00 PM

From Saturday and Sunday: 1:00 PM - 6:00 PM

Cost of Entrance:

General Admission: €9 (approximately $10)

Reduced Admission: €5 (approximately $5.50) for students, seniors, and groups

Free for children under 18 and for everyone on the first Sunday of the month

Parks and Gardens

Lille boasts a variety of beautiful parks and gardens, offering serene spots for relaxation, recreation, and enjoying nature. Here are some of the top green spaces you should visit in the city.

- Parc de la Citadelle

Located at Avenue du 43e Régiment d'Infanterie, 59800 Lille, France

The largest park in Lille, Parc de la Citadelle, surrounds the historic Lille Citadel. It's a popular spot for locals and visitors alike, offering a blend of natural beauty and historical significance.

The park encompasses the impressive star-shaped citadel designed by Vauban.

The park includes playgrounds, a zoo, and extensive paths for walking, running, and cycling.

It has Large lawns, wooded areas, and beautiful flower beds that make it an ideal place for picnics and strolls.

Open daily from 8:00 AM to 8:00 PM

Cost of Entry: Free

- Jardin Vauban

Located at Boulevard de la Liberté, 59000 Lille, France

A picturesque park inspired by English gardens, Jardin Vauban is known for its winding paths, romantic groves, and charming water features.

Several statues and monuments are scattered throughout the garden.

Opens from 7:30 AM to 7:30 PM on a daily basis

Cost of Entry: Free

- Parc Jean-Baptiste Lebas

Located at Rue de Cambrai, 59000 Lille, France

This modern urban park is a vibrant green space featuring a mix of lawns, playgrounds, and cultural installations, making it a lively community hub.

The park is famously bordered by striking red gates it Includes areas for children's play, as well as spaces for sports and relaxation.

Frequently hosts events, performances, and exhibitions.

Opens from 8:00 AM to 8:00 PM on a daily basis

Cost of Entry: Free

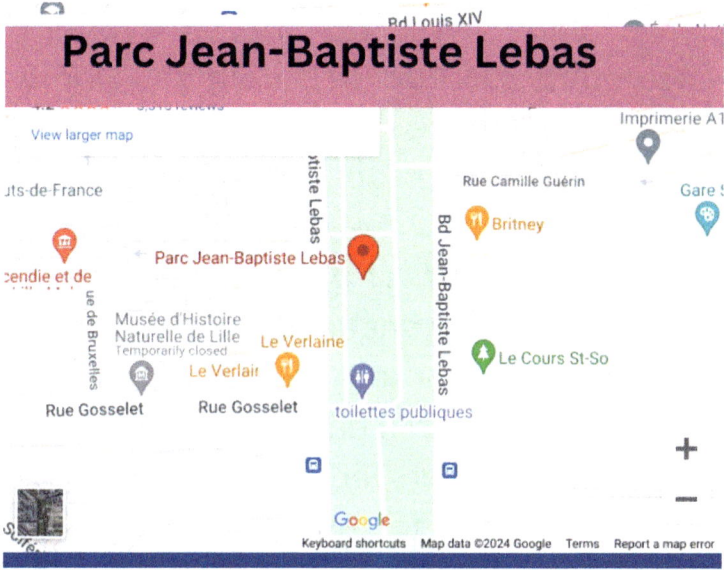

Parc Jean-Baptiste Lebas

How To Scan The QR Code

- Ensure your smartphone has a camera.
- Open the Camera App,you don't need any special settings the regular photo mode will often work.
- Aim your camera at the QR code. Make sure the QR code is clearly visible within the camera's frame.
- Hold your device steady while the camera focuses on the QR code. most camera apps will recognize the QR code automatically and process it within a few seconds.
- Follow the Prompt

92

- Jardin des Plantes

Located at 306 Rue du Jardin des Plantes, 59000 Lille, France

A botanical garden with a rich collection of plants, trees, and flowers, the Jardin des Plantes is perfect for plant enthusiasts and those seeking a tranquil environment.

This garden houses exotic plants and serves as a research and education center.

This garden offers educational programs and guided tours for visitors.

Opens from 8:00 AM to 7:00 PM daily

Cost of Entry: Free

- Parc Henri Matisse

Located at Boulevard Louis XIV, 59800 Lille, France

Located near the Lille Europe railway station, this modern park offers open spaces, artistic installations, and panoramic views of the city. It Provides elevated views of the cityscape and the nearby railway station.

Opens from 8:00 AM to 8:00 PM on a daily basis

Cost of Entry: Free

Shopping and Food Markets

Lille's food markets are vibrant and bustling places where you can experience the city's culinary diversity and fresh, local produce. From traditional markets to gourmet food stalls, these markets are a great way to taste local flavors and interact with the community.

- Grand Place

An impressive square in the heart of Lille!, also known as Place du Général de Gaulle, but everyone calls it the Grand Place meaning a big place. The grand place is always crowded because different people meet up here.

There are many restaurants, and check the architecture of the buildings and the statue of the goddess in the center of the square, built in 1842.

There is a Ferris wheel on the grand place during Christmas.

Location: Place du Général de Gaulle, 59800 Lille, France

Opening Hours: Open 24 hours; however, the best time to visit is during the day when the shops and cafes are open.

Cost of Entry: Free

- Rue de Béthune

Location: Rue de Béthune, 59800 Lille, France

Rue de Béthune is one of Lille's premier shopping streets, offering a lively pedestrian-friendly area filled with shops, eateries, and entertainment options. This bustling street is a favorite among locals and tourists alike for its vibrant atmosphere and diverse offerings.

The street is lined with international brands and local boutiques, providing a diverse shopping experience. You'll find everything from fashion and footwear to electronics and books.

Several cinemas, including UGC and Majestic, make Rue de Béthune a popular spot for catching the latest films. There are also occasional street performances and events that add to the lively ambiance.

Opening Hours:

Shops are generally open from 10:00 AM to 7:00 PM, Monday to Saturday. Many shops are closed on Sundays, although some cafes and cinemas remain open.

Cost of Entry: Free; however, prices for goods and services vary by establishment.

- Marché de Wazemmes

The Marché de Wazemmes is one of Lille's most popular and diverse markets, offering different food products and local specialties.

The market sells fresh fruits, vegetables, meats, cheeses, and baked goods, alongside international foods and spices.

Located at Place de la Nouvelle Aventure, 59000 Lille, France

Opening Hours:

Tuesday, Thursday, and Sunday: 7:00 AM - 2:00 PM

Cost: Entry is free but prices of goods vary by vendor.

it is a popular place, don't miss it!

- **Marché du Vieux-Lille**

Located in the historic district of Vieux-Lille, this market Focuses on high-quality, locally-made products, including cheeses, charcuterie, pastries, and jams.

Location: Rue de la Monnaie, 59800 Lille, France

Opening Hours:

Just Wednesday and Saturday: 8:00 AM - 1:00 PM

Cost: Entry is free but prices of goods vary by vendor.

- **Marché de Fives**

This local market is a favorite among residents for its range of fresh produce and affordable prices.

Location: Place Roger Salengro, 59800 Lille, France

Opening Hours:

Tuesday, Thursday, and Saturday: 7:00 AM - 1:00 PM

Cost: Entry is free; prices vary by vendor.

- **Marché de la Gare**

Location: Rue du Pont Neuf, 59000 Lille, France

This smaller market near Lille's train station is ideal for picking fresh produce and gourmet items before traveling.

Opening Hours:

Monday to Saturday: 8:00 AM - 1:00 PM

Cost: Entry is free; prices vary by vendor.

Chapter Six: What do they eat in Lille and where to get the best meal

Traditional Dishes

Lille's dishes are a delightful blend of French finesse and Flemish heartiness, offering a rich combination of flavors and textures. The city's traditional dishes reflect its unique cultural heritage and are a must-try for any food lover.

- Carbonnade Flamande

Carbonnade Flamande is a hearty beef stew made with onions and Belgian beer, thyme, juniper berries, mustard, and spiced bread, often served with potatoes or fries. This dish is perfect for warming up on a chilly day.

- Moules-Frites

A classic dish from the region, Moules-Frites consists of mussels cooked in sauces (commonly white wine, cream, and garlic) and served with crispy fries.

The mussels are usually sourced fresh from the North Sea, ensuring a delectable taste of the sea.

- Potjevleesch

Potjevleesch, which means "potted meat" in Flemish, is a terrine made of three or four different meats (typically chicken, rabbit, and pork) in gelatin. It is often served cold with fries and salad.

The meats are cooked with herbs and spices and then set in their gelatin, creating a savory, rich dish.

- Welsh Rarebit

A local twist on the British classic, Welsh Rarebit in Lille involves melted cheese, beer, ham, and mustard, served over toasted bread.

- Tarte au Maroilles

Tarte au Maroilles is a savory tart made with Maroilles cheese, a strong-smelling but delicious cheese from the region.

- Waterzooi

Originally from Belgium but popular in Lille, Waterzooi is a creamy stew made with fish or chicken, vegetables, and a rich broth of egg yolks, cream, and butter.

Best Restaurants and Cafés

1. La Petite Cour

Address: 17 Rue du Cure St-Etienne, 59800, Lille France

This elegant restaurant has a blend of both French and European dishes.

There are vegetarian/Vegan dishes Options

Opening Hours:

Monday to Saturday: 12:00 PM - 2:00 PM, 7:00 PM - 11:300 PM

Closed Sunday

Cost: Expect to spend around €10-€40 ($12.00 – $55.00) per person, depending on the dishes ordered.

2. Le Barbue d'Anvers

Address: 1bis Rue Saint-Etienne, 59800 Lille, France

Le Barbue d'Anvers offers traditional Flemish cuisine in a cozy, medieval-style setting. The restaurant is famous for its hearty dishes and charming atmosphere.

The interior is decorated with medieval artifacts, wooden beams, and warm lighting, creating a rustic and inviting atmosphere.

Opening Hours:

Monday to Saturday: 12:00 PM - 2:30 PM, 7:00 PM - 10:30 PM

Closed Sunday

Cost: Approximately €25-€50 ($28-$57) per person.

3. La Chicorée

Address: 15 Place Rihour, 59800 Lille, France

La Chicorée is a popular brasserie in the heart of Lille, offering a wide range of French and regional dishes in a lively atmosphere.

offers a diverse menu with everything from traditional French cuisine to regional specialties and international dishes.

It is also One of the few places in Lille open late, making it a great option for late-night meals.

Opening Hours is from 8:00 AM to 2:00 AM daily

Cost: Around €20-€40 ($23-$46) per person.

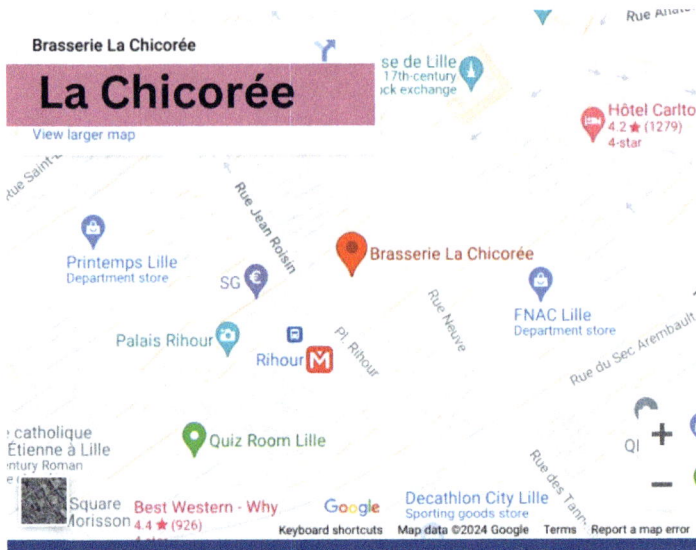

Brasserie La Chicorée

La Chicorée

View larger map

How To Scan The QR Code

- Ensure your smartphone has a camera.
- Open the Camera App,you don't need any special settings the regular photo mode will often work.
- Aim your camera at the QR code. Make sure the QR code is clearly visible within the camera's frame.
- Hold your device steady while the camera focuses on the QR code. most camera apps will recognize the QR code automatically and process it within a few seconds.
- Follow the Prompt

107

4. Bloempot

Located at 22 Rue des Bouchers, 59800 Lille, France

Bloempot offers a unique dining experience with its focus on contemporary Flemish cuisine. The restaurant is housed in a former factory, giving it an industrial-chic vibe.

The menu features creative dishes putting a modern twist on traditional Flemish flavors.

They offer special diets Vegetarian Friendly, Vegan Options

Opening Hours:

Wednesday to Saturday: 12:00 PM - 2:00 PM, 7:00 PM - 10:00 PM

Closed Sunday to Monday

Cost: Expect to spend €40-€70 ($46-$80) per person.

5. Méert

Address: 27 Rue Esquermoise, 59800 Lille, France

Méert is a historic pâtisserie and café known for its pastries and elegant tearoom. Here you need to taste their waffles filled with vanilla from Madagascar! Tastes So Yummy.

Meert is first opened in 1849

Opening Hours:

From Tuesday to Saturday: 9:00 AM - 7:30 PM

Sunday: 10:00 AM - 7:00 PM

Closed Monday

Cost: Pastries and desserts range from €5-€15 ($6-$17); tea service and light meals around €20-€30 ($23-$35) per person.

6 . La Capsule

Located at 25 Rue des trois Mollettes, 59800 Lille, France

This is a Craft Beer Pub. It is a nice spot for beer Lovers.

Though it is not the cheapest, their goods are not overpriced.

located in a relaxed atmosphere.

There is no option for dinner, but they have nice snacks.
Cost: $3.00 – $11.00
Opening hours are from 6:30 PM - 1:00 AM

7 . Le Bistrot
40 Rue de Gand, 59800, Lille France
A busy restaurant with French and European cuisine
Opening hours: Sun - Saturday
12:00 PM - 3:00 PM
6:00 PM - 10:00 PM
Cost ranges from $30.00 – $37.00

Chapter Seven: Cultural Experiences and Nightlife

Festivals and Events

Lille's cultural scene is enriched by its numerous festivals and events held throughout the year.

Some of the Festival and Events are

- La Grande Braderie de Lille

One of Europe's largest flea markets, La Grande Braderie de Lille is an annual event that transforms the city into a massive marketplace.

Over 10,000 vendors sell a diverse range of items, from antiques and vintage clothing to books and collectibles.

it attracts more than two million people!

Dates: First weekend of September

Location: Throughout Lille, primarily around the Grand Place and Vieux-Lille

Cost: Free entry but prices of goods vary by vendor.

- **Lille Piano(s) Festival**

A celebration of piano music featuring performances by renowned pianists and emerging talents.

Venues: Held in various locations around Lille, including concert halls and cultural centers.

Dates: Annually in April

Cost: Ticket prices range from €10-€30 ($12-$35), depending on the performance.

- **Lille3000**

A major cultural event held every three years, Lille3000 is a city-wide festival celebrating arts, culture, and creativity.

Dates: Biennial event, typically held from October to February

Location: Various locations across Lille

Cost: Entry fees vary by event; many activities are free.

- Festival de Lille

A general arts festival celebrating a wide range of cultural activities, including music, theater, dance, and visual arts.
Dates: Various times throughout the year
Location: Various venues in Lille
Cost: Ticket prices range from €10-€50 ($12-$57), depending on the event.

- Marché de Noël

Lille's Christmas market is a festive event that transforms the city into a winter wonderland.
Features over 80 stalls selling holiday gifts, decorations, and festive foods.
Dates: Late November to late December
Location: Place Rihour, Lille, France
Cost: Free entry; prices vary by vendor.

- Lille Opera House.

Address: 2 rue des Bons Enfants, 59001, Lille France

The Opera is located in the very center of the old town and is a must to visit there if the Opera is on or just to see the beautiful and recently renovated interior

Quality singing and productions in a great theater. It is 6 min walk from Gare Lille Flandres

Opening hours: Tuesday- Saturday; 12:00 PM - 7:00 PM

Music and Nightlife

Lille's music and nightlife scene is as dynamic as the city itself, offering a range of experiences from lively bars and clubs to intimate music venues.

- Le Magazine Club

Address: 84 Rue de Trévise, 59100 Lille, France

A popular nightclub known for its energetic atmosphere and top-notch DJs, Le

Magazine Club is a hotspot for nightlife enthusiasts.

Opening Hours:

Friday and Saturday from 11:00 PM - 6:00 AM

Closed Sunday to Thursday

Cost: The entry fee is typically around €10-€20 ($12-$23), depending on the event.

- L'Aeronef

A renowned live music venue in Lille, L'Aeronef hosts a wide range of performances from local and international artists.

Address: 108 Boulevard de Lille, 59777 Lille, France

Opening Hours:

Varies depending on event times

Cost: Ticket prices range from €15-€35 ($17-$40), depending on the performance.

- Le Bar de la Bourse

A lively bar known for its relaxed atmosphere and live music sessions, Le Bar de la Bourse is a favorite among locals.

Address: 2 Place du Général de Gaulle, 59800 Lille, France

Opening Hours:

Monday to Saturday from 11:00 AM - 1:00 AM

Closed Sunday

Cost: Drinks and snacks range from €5-€15 ($6-$17).

- La Péniche

An alternative music venue located on a boat moored on the Deûle River, La Péniche offers a unique and charming setting for live music.

Address: 1 avenue Cuvier, 59800, Lille France

Opening Hours:

Varies depending on event times

Cost: Ticket prices typically range from €10-€20 ($12-$23), depending on the performance.

La Péniche

4.2 ★★★★ ☆ 3,445 reviews

View larger map

FFIA Charging Station

Parking Liberté - Métropole...

Av. du 43E RI

Monument aux Pigeons Voyageurs

Lille Citadelle

Le Bus Magique
Vegetarian

Sq-Daubeton

...in d'Eau Douce Lille Da

I de la
e-Deûle

M750

Bro's Bar & Burger

Péniche Archimède

Péniche Aristote

Rue Léonard Danel

Église S

Rue du Gros Gérard

La Clé du Barb
- VIEUX LILLE

Rue de

Sia Habitat

Quai du Wault

Hôtel Couvent
Des Minimes
4.1 ★ (1154)
4-star

M750 Google

Keyboard shortcuts   Map data ©2024 Google   Terms   Report a map error

How To Scan The QR Code

- Ensure your smartphone has a camera.
- Open the Camera App,you don't need any special settings the regular photo mode will often work.
- Aim your camera at the QR code. Make sure the QR code is clearly visible within the camera's frame.
- Hold your device steady while the camera focuses on the QR code. most camera apps will recognize the QR code automatically and process it within a few seconds.
- Follow the Prompt

118

- La Nuit du Folk

A festival dedicated to folk music, La Nuit du Folk offers a night of traditional and contemporary folk performances in a lively setting.

Address: Various venues in Lille

Opening Hours:

Typically runs from 7:00 PM - 2:00 AM

Cost: Ticket prices generally range from €10-€25 ($12-$29), depending on the lineup.

Local Customs and Etiquette

Understanding local customs and etiquette will enhance your experience in Lille and help you connect with the community.

Greeting and Politeness

Greetings: A handshake is the most common form of greeting, but close friends and family may greet each other with a kiss on both cheeks.

Politeness: Use polite phrases such as "s'il vous plaît" (please) and "merci" (thank you). It's appreciated when you make an effort to use French, even if it's just a few words.

Tipping

In France, a service charge is included in your bill, so tipping is not obligatory but appreciated. Rounding up the bill or leaving a small amount (around 5-10%) is a nice gesture for good service.

Public Behavior

In public spaces, such as public transport or cafes, it's polite to keep conversations at a moderate volume. Loud behavior is generally frowned upon.

Maintain a respectful distance in queues and when interacting with others.

Shopping and Markets

While bargaining is not common in most shops and supermarkets, it's acceptable in some markets. Approach it politely and be prepared for a friendly negotiation.

Many shops close for a lunch break from around 12:00 PM to 2:00 PM. Be aware of this when planning your shopping trips.

Money Saving Tip

If you can time your trip over the 1st Sunday of the month, entry to the Palais des Beaux-Arts, Musée d'Histoire Naturelle and Musée de l'Hospice Comtesse are all completely free.

Chapter Eight: Safety Tips

When traveling to Lille, it is essential to stay safe and healthy to ensure an enjoyable trip. Lille is generally a safe city for travelers, but it's always wise to take common precautions to ensure a pleasant trip.

Here are some practical safety and health tips to keep in mind:

General Safety Tips:

1 . Stay Aware of Your Surroundings

Like in any city, be mindful of your belongings and surroundings, especially in crowded areas like markets and public transportation.

2 . Avoid solitary or dark areas at night.

When you stroll at night, stay in crowded, well-lit areas. Try to go in groups if you can, or make use of dependable modes of transportation like ride-sharing or taxis.

3. Preserve Priceless Items

To protect your belongings, choose a tight bag or a money belt.

4 . Know Emergency Contacts

Familiarize yourself with local emergency numbers.

5 . Respect Local Customs

Being aware of local customs and etiquette can help you avoid misunderstandings and enjoy a more respectful interaction with locals.

Health Tips

1 . Stay Hydrated

2 . Food Safety

Enjoy Lille's culinary delights, but ensure that food from street vendors and markets is freshly prepared and cooked thoroughly. Opt for bottled water if you're unsure about tap water quality.

3 . Personal Medications

Bring any necessary medications with you, along with a copy of your prescriptions. It's also helpful to have a basic first aid kit on hand for minor injuries.

4 . Investing in comprehensive travel insurance that covers health, accidents, and trip cancellations will give you

financial security and peace of mind in the event of an emergency.

5. COVID-19 Precautions: Stay informed about the most recent health guidelines and travel advisories related to COVID-19. You can find the most up-to-date information on official government websites.

6 . Mask and Sanitation

Carry a face mask and hand sanitizer. Use them in crowded places, on public transport, and where local regulations require.

7 . Vaccination and Testing

Ensure you meet the vaccination or testing requirements for entry into France and any venues or attractions you plan to visit.

Local Healthcare

1 . Pharmacies

Pharmacies are readily available in Lille and can provide over-the-counter medications and health advice. Look for a green cross sign to identify them.

2 . Medical Services: In case of illness or injury, Lille has excellent healthcare facilities.

3 . Language Assistance: While many healthcare professionals in Lille speak English, it can be helpful to have basic French phrases or a translation app to communicate medical needs.

Transportation Safety:

1 . Public Transportation

The public transportation system in Lille is typically reliable and effective but you should keep an eye on your belongings, especially during peak hours.

2 . Road Safety

Recognize the laws and ordinances governing traffic in your area before driving. Avoid using your phone while driving and always buckle up.

3 . Bike Safety

If renting a bike, use designated bike lanes where possible and wear a helmet for safety.

Local Laws and Emergency Contacts

Understanding local laws and knowing emergency contacts is crucial for a safe and trouble-free visit to Lille.

Identity: Make sure you always have some sort of identification on you. Hold a photocopy of your passport or another form of identification even though it's best to keep it in a safe location.

Alcohol Use: In France, the legal drinking age is eighteen. Drinking in public places is generally allowed, but be mindful of local regulations and respect public decency laws.

Smoking: Smoking is banned in public places, including restaurants, bars, and public transport. Look for designated smoking areas.

Drugs: The use, possession, and trafficking of illegal drugs are strictly prohibited and can result in severe penalties.

Public Conduct: Honor regional traditions and cultural standards. While showing affection in public is typically appropriate, going overboard may not be. Refrain from being noisy or unruly in public areas.

Traffic Rules: If you're driving, abide by the applicable local traffic rules. It is against the law to use a cell phone while driving unless you have a hands-free system installed, and seatbelts are required.

Respect for Property: Public and private property should be treated with respect. Graffiti and vandalism are prohibited and subject to legal penalties.

Emergency Contacts: Lille is a generally safe city that is easy to navigate and walk in. There is a low crime rate, making it a safe place for residents, tourists, and single visitors alike.

Here is a list of the contacts you'll need in Lille in case of emergency:

European emergency number: 112

Ambulance service: 15

Fire service: 18

Police: 17
Police station in Lille: +33362598000
Gendarme station: +33320169696

Chapter Nine: Practical Information

Language and Useful Phrases

French is the official language spoken in Lille. While many locals, especially in the service and tourism sectors, speak some English, it's always appreciated when visitors make an effort to speak a few words of French. Knowing some basic phrases can greatly enhance your experience and interactions with the locals.

Useful Phrases

Greetings and Basics:

Hello: Bonjour (bohn-zhoor)

Good evening: Bonsoir (bohn-swahr)

Goodbye: Au revoir (oh ruh-vwahr)

Please: S'il vous plaît (seel voo pleh)

Thank you: Merci (mehr-see)

Yes: Oui (wee)

No: Non (noh)

Introductions:

My name is...: Je m'appelle... (zhuh mah-pehl)

What is your name?: Comment vous appelez-vous? (koh-mahn voo zah-pehl-eh voo)

Nice to meet you: Enchanté (ahn-shahn-tay)

Getting Around:

Where is...?: Où est...? (oo eh)

How do I get to...?: Comment puis-je aller à...? (koh-mahn pwee-zh ah-lay ah)

Train station: Gare (Gahr)

Bus stop: Arrêt de bus (ah-reh duh boos)

Left: Gauche (gosh)

Right: Droite (drwaht)

Straight ahead: Tout droit (to drwa)

Eating Out:

I would like...: Je voudrais... (zhuh voo-dray)

The bill, please: L'addition, s'il vous plaît (lah-dee-syon, seel voo pleh)

Water: Eau (oh)

Coffee: Café (kah-fay)

Wine: Vin (van)

Shopping:

How much is this?: Combien ça coûte? (kohm-byen sah koot)

Do you have...?: Avez-vous...? (ah-vay voo)

Open: Ouvert (oo-vehr)

Closed: Fermé (fehr-may)

Emergency:

Help!: Au secours! (oh suh-koor)

I need a doctor: J'ai besoin d'un médecin (zhay buh-zwan dun mayd-sahn)

Police: Police (poh-lees)

Hospital: Hôpital (oh-pee-tal)

Tips for Communication

Politeness: Always greet with "Bonjour" before asking for help or information. French people appreciate polite manners.

Even if your French is not perfect, making an effort goes a long way in showing respect and can lead to warmer interactions.

If someone is speaking too quickly, you can say "Parlez lentement, s'il vous plaît"

(Par-lay lahnt-moh, seel voo pleh), which means "Please speak slowly."

By learning and using these simple phrases, you'll find it easier to navigate Lille and connect with its residents, making your travel experience more enjoyable and immersive

Currency and Banking in Lille

Lille, like the rest of France, uses the Euro (€) as its official currency. Banknotes come in denominations of €5, €10, €20, €50, €100, €200, and €500, while coins are available in 1, 2, 5, 10, 20, and 50 cents, and €1 and €2.

Exchanging Money

You can exchange money at banks, which are usually open from 9:00 AM to 5:00 PM, Monday to Friday, with some branches open on Saturday mornings.

Exchange bureaus in the city center and at the train stations offer convenient services, often with longer hours.

ATMs: Automated Teller Machines (ATMs) are widely available throughout Lille. They accept major international cards such as Visa, MasterCard, and American Express.

How to Use Debit and Credit Cards

Hotels, restaurants, stores, and a lot of attractions accept credit and debit cards. But it's always a good idea to have some cash on hand, particularly for marketplaces and smaller businesses.

Chip-and-PIN: France uses the chip-and-PIN system for credit and debit card transactions. Make sure your card has a chip and know your PIN code.

Currency Conversion Fees: Be aware of potential currency conversion fees charged by your bank when using your card abroad. Check with your bank before traveling to understand any applicable charges.

Banking Services: Tax Refunds for Tourists

Non-EU residents can claim a refund on the Value Added Tax (VAT) for goods purchased in France, provided the total amount spent in one store exceeds €100.01. Look for stores displaying the "Tax-Free Shopping" sign and ask for a tax refund form (bordereau de détaxe).

When leaving the EU, present your completed tax refund forms, receipts, and purchased goods to customs officials at the airport or train station. After validation, you can claim your refund at the airport's tax refund office or have it processed by mail.

Emergency Cash

Lost or Stolen Cards: If your card is lost or stolen, contact your bank immediately to report it and request a replacement. Keep your bank's international emergency contact number handy.

If you need emergency cash, you can get a cash advance from your credit card at most banks and ATMs.

Internet and Communication

Internet Access

Wi-Fi is widely available in Lille, with many hotels, cafes, restaurants, and public spaces offering free access. Most establishments will provide you with the Wi-Fi password upon request.

Public Wi-Fi: The city offers free public Wi-Fi in various locations, including main squares, parks, and libraries. Look for signs indicating Wi-Fi zones.

Internet Cafes: While not as common as they once were, internet cafes can still be found in Lille. They offer computer and internet access for a fee, which is useful if you need to print documents or use a computer.

Mobile Connectivity

If you plan to stay in Lille for an extended period, consider purchasing a local SIM card. Major mobile providers like Orange,

SFR, Bouygues Telecom, and Free Mobile offer prepaid SIM cards that can be easily topped up.

You can buy SIM cards at mobile provider stores, electronics shops, and even at some supermarkets and newsstands. SIM cards are also available at Lille's main train stations and the airport.

Prepaid SIM cards typically start at around €10-€20, with various data and call packages available. Prior to buying a local SIM card, make sure your phone is unlocked.

Using Your Home Mobile Plan

Roaming: Many providers offer international roaming packages that include calls, texts, and data usage in France, but these can be expensive without a specific plan.

EU Roaming Regulations: If you have a mobile plan from another EU country, you can use your phone in Lille without incurring additional roaming charges due to EU regulations.

Communication Apps

Apps like WhatsApp, Telegram, and Viber are widely used for messaging and voice calls. Ensure you have these apps installed and set up before you travel.

For video calls, apps like Zoom, Skype, and FaceTime are popular and can help you stay connected with friends and family back home.

Language Assistance Apps

Apps like Google Translate and iTranslate can be incredibly useful for translating French to your native language and vice versa. These apps often include voice translation features, which can be handy for quick conversations.

Phrasebook Apps: Consider downloading a French phrasebook app to help you with basic phrases and pronunciation.

Postal Services

Post Offices: La Poste is

France's national postal service and you can find post offices throughout Lille. They usually operate from 9:00 AM to 6:00 PM, Monday to Friday, with some branches open on Saturday mornings.

You can send letters and parcels domestically and internationally from any post office. Stamps (timbres) can be purchased at post offices, tabacs (tobacco shops), and some newsstands.

Postboxes: Yellow post boxes (boîtes aux lettres) are located throughout the city for mailing letters.

Staying Connected

Local Contacts: Make sure to have the contact details of your accommodation, tour operators, and any local friends or contacts saved in your phone.

Backup Battery: Carry a portable battery charger to keep your devices powered up while exploring the city.

Public Holidays

Some major public holidays in Lille include New Year's Day (January 1), Easter Monday (date varies), Labor Day (May 1), Bastille Day (July 14), and Christmas Day (December 25).

On public holidays, most businesses, banks, and public offices are closed, though some tourist attractions and restaurants may remain open.

Understanding Lille's time zone and business hours will help you plan your activities and ensure you make the most of your visit.

Travel Insurance

Why You Need Travel Insurance

Travel insurance is essential for any trip, including your visit to Lille. It provides coverage for unexpected events and emergencies, ensuring peace of mind and financial protection. Here's a rundown of why travel insurance is important and what it typically covers:

Types of Coverage

1 . Medical Emergencies: Covers medical expenses for illnesses or injuries sustained during your trip. Hospital stays, doctor visits, and emergency medical evacuations might be included.

2 . Trip Cancellation: Reimburses you for prepaid, non-refundable expenses if you need to cancel your trip due to unforeseen circumstances such as illness, a family emergency, or other covered reasons.

3 . Trip Interruption: This covers additional expenses if your trip is cut short due to an emergency, allowing you to return home earlier than planned.

4 . Lost or Stolen Belongings: Provides reimbursement for lost, stolen, or damaged personal items, including luggage, electronics, and travel documents.

5 . Travel Delays: Covers expenses incurred due to significant travel delays, such as accommodation, meals, and transportation.

6 . Personal Liability: Protects you in case you are held legally responsible for causing injury to someone or damage to their property.

Choosing the Right Travel Insurance

Consider the following factors when selecting a travel insurance:

1 . Coverage Limits: Ensure the policy covers all potential costs, including high medical expenses and evacuation costs.

2 . Exclusions: Be aware of any exclusions in the policy, such as pre-existing medical conditions or activities considered high-risk (e.g., extreme sports).

3 . Duration: Make sure the policy covers the entire duration of your trip, from departure to return.

4 . Cost: Compare prices and coverage options from multiple providers to find the best value for your needs.

5 . Provider Reputation: Choose a reputable insurance company with good customer reviews and reliable customer service.

Where to Buy Travel Insurance

1 . Travel Agencies: Many travel agencies offer travel insurance as part of their service packages.

2 . Insurance Companies: You can purchase travel insurance directly from insurance companies, either online or through their customer service centers.

3 . Credit Card Providers: Some credit cards offer complimentary travel insurance when you use the card to book your trip.

Claim Process

Documentation: Keep all receipts, medical reports, and police reports related to your claim.

Contact Information: Note the emergency contact number for your insurance provider, and know the procedure for making a claim.

Timely Reporting: Report any incidents to your insurance provider as soon as possible to avoid complications or denial of coverage.

Chapter Ten: Day Trips and Excursions

Surrounding Towns and Villages

Exploring beyond Lille offers a chance to discover charming towns and picturesque villages, each with its unique character and attractions. Here are some must-visit destinations for day trips from Lille:

Roubaix

Just a short train ride from Lille, Roubaix is known for its rich industrial heritage and impressive cultural sites. The star attraction is La Piscine Museum. Don't miss the vibrant atmosphere of the Grand Place and the bustling market days.

Roubaix

How To Scan The QR Code

- Ensure your smartphone has a camera.
- Open the Camera App, you don't need any special settings the regular photo mode will often work.
- Aim your camera at the QR code. Make sure the QR code is clearly visible within the camera's frame.
- Hold your device steady while the camera focuses on the QR code. most camera apps will recognize the QR code automatically and process it within a few seconds.
- Follow the Prompt

Arras

Arras, an hour's drive from Lille, boasts beautiful Flemish-Baroque architecture and a history that dates back to Roman times.

The town's twin squares, Grand' Place and Place des Héros are surrounded by elegant townhouses and lively cafes. The Belfry of Arras offers panoramic views, and the underground tunnels of the Boves provide a fascinating glimpse into the town's past. Visit the Arras Memorial and the Wellington Quarry for a sobering reminder of World War I history.

Cassel

Perched on a hilltop about an hour's drive from Lille, Cassel offers breathtaking views of the surrounding countryside. Visit the Musée de Flandre for a deep dive into Flemish culture, and enjoy the peaceful ambiance of the Jardin du Mont des Récollets. The village's traditional windmill and charming cafes add to its appeal, making it a perfect spot for a relaxing day out.

Ypres (Ieper), Belgium

A short trip across the border, Ypres is a city steeped in history, particularly from

World War I. Visit the In Flanders Fields Museum to understand the profound impact of the war, and attend the moving Last Post ceremony at the Menin Gate, held every evening at 8 PM. Explore the medieval architecture, including the Cloth Hall and St. Martin's Cathedral, and take a stroll around the well-preserved city ramparts.

Tournai, Belgium

Another easy cross-border excursion, Tournai is one of Belgium's oldest cities. Marvel at the UNESCO-listed Notre-Dame Cathedral with its five distinctive bell towers, and climb the Belfry for stunning views over the city. The Museum of Fine Arts, designed by Victor Horta, houses an impressive collection of works by artists such as Rubens and Manet. The quaint streets, historic sites, and cozy cafes make Tournai a delightful day trip destination.

Conclusion

As you close the pages of this guide, the essence of Lille lingers, a city where every corner tells a story. Lille's beauty lies in its historic landmarks, the buzz of vibrant markets balanced by serene parks, and the warmth of its people expressing their lovely culture.

Whether you are walking through the streets of Vieux Lille, indulging in the rich flavors of Flemish cuisine, or marveling at masterpieces in the Palais des Beaux-Arts, Lille has offered you a taste of its soul, Lille invites you to discover its hidden gems, to engage with its local life, and to let its spirit resonate within you.

As you are done going through this guide it is time to journey in and around Lille.

And after exploring and about leaving, you leave not just with memories, but with the feeling of having experienced a city that is both welcoming and enigmatic. Lille is a destination that doesn't just show you its beauty; it shares its heart, ensuring that no matter where you go next, a part of Lille goes with you.

Resources

Useful Apps and Websites.

Google Maps: Essential for navigating Lille and discovering local attractions, restaurants, and amenities.

Citymapper: A great app for planning public transport routes within Lille, including buses, metro, and trams.

TripAdvisor: Useful for finding reviews and recommendations for restaurants, attractions, and hotels.

Duolingo: Helpful for brushing up on basic French phrases and language skills before and during your trip.

Lille City Pass: The official app for the Lille City Pass, which offers access to multiple attractions and discounts.

****

I hope you have enjoyed the journey within the pages of my book. Your thoughts and feedback are invaluable to me, and I would love to hear about your experience.

If my book has resonated with you, inspired new perspectives, or simply brought joy to your reading moments, please consider leaving a review on Amazon. Your words have the power to reach fellow readers and make a significant impact. Your honest review will not only provide insights for potential readers but also help my book gain visibility in the vast world of literature. Every review is a meaningful contribution that I truly appreciate. Thank you.

****

Bonus Corner

7-days Itinerary for Lille and Surroundings

After you have arrived at Lille, and settled down in your accommodation.

The next thing that comes to your mind will be "Oh yeah! It is time to explore this wonderful city".

Do not rush it. Just take a rest and continue the next day.

This itinerary I am giving you is just a suggested itinerary, you can plan yours depending on the number of days you want to stay and also places you wish to visit.

If you plan to stay up to 7- days, then you can consider using this one in this book.

Day 1: Exploring Lille

- **Morning**

Grand Place: Start your trip with a visit to the heart of Lille, the Grand Place. Marvel at the architecture and vibrant atmosphere.

Vieille Bourse: Explore the Old Stock Exchange, an architectural gem with a beautiful courtyard and book market.

- **Afternoon**

Visit Palais des Beaux-Arts, one of the largest fine arts museums in France, showcasing a vast collection of European paintings and sculptures.

Lunch at La Chicorée and Enjoy traditional Flemish dishes at this popular local restaurant.

- **Evening**

Stroll through the charming streets of Old Lille(Vieux Lille), lined with boutiques, cafes, and historic buildings.

Dinner at Bloempot, Dine at this trendy restaurant that offers innovative French dishes.

Day 2: Culture and History

- **Morning**

Explore Lille Citadel and walk around the surrounding park.

Discover an extensive collection of modern and contemporary art at LaM

- **Afternoon**

Enjoy Lunch at Estaminet 'T Rijsel, Savor traditional Flemish cuisine in a cozy setting.

Learn about the history of Lille through its collection of artworks and artifacts in a former hospital Hospice Comtesse Museum.

- **Evening**

If available, attend a performance at the beautiful Lille Opera House.

Enjoy a fine dinner in a historic hotel setting L'Hermitage Gantois.

Day 3: Day Trip to Roubaix

- Morning

Visit this unique museum set at La Piscine Museum, featuring fine arts and textile exhibits.

- Afternoon

Enjoy lunch and pastries at Meert.

Shopping at McArthurGlen Designer Outlet:

- Evening

Return to Lille: Relax at your hotel or explore more of Lille's nightlife.

Day 4: Discovering Arras

- Morning

Grand Place and Place des Héros: Wander through the picturesque squares of Arras, lined with Flemish-Baroque buildings.

- Afternoon

Lunch at Le Clusius: Enjoy a meal in the heart of Arras.

Arras Belfry: Climb the belfry for panoramic views of the town.

Wellington Quarry: Visit this historical site to learn about the underground tunnels used during WWI.

- Evening

Return to Lille: Dine at any local restaurant of your choice and enjoy a leisurely evening.

Day 5: Nature and Relaxation

- Morning

Parc du Héron: Spend the morning exploring this beautiful park in Villeneuve d'Ascq. Walk or bike around the lake and enjoy the natural surroundings.

- Afternoon

Lunch at Le Bistro du Lac: Enjoy lakeside dining with a view.

LaM Park: Visit the nearby LaM Park for a relaxing stroll among outdoor sculptures.

- Evening

Dinner at Au Bistrot de la Grand Place: Delight in traditional French cuisine in a charming setting.

Day 6: Cross-Border Excursion to Ypres, Belgium

- **Morning**

In Flanders Fields Museum: Explore this poignant museum dedicated to the history of WWI.

- **Afternoon**

Lunch at Het Moment: Enjoy a meal in a historic building with a peaceful garden.

Menin Gate and Ramparts: Walk around the city's medieval ramparts and visit the Menin Gate Memorial.

- **Evening**

Attend the moving Last Post ceremony at the Menin Gate, held every evening at 8 PM.

Return to Lille: Have a late dinner at a local bistro.

Day 7: Leisure and Shopping

- **Morning**

Experience the vibrant Wazemmes Market, filled with fresh produce, local specialties, and a lively atmosphere.

- **Afternoon**

Lunch at La Capsule: Relax with a drink and a light meal at this popular craft beer bar.

Rue de Béthune: Spend the afternoon shopping along this bustling pedestrian street, home to numerous boutiques and stores.

- **Evening**

Farewell Dinner at La Petite Cour: End your trip with a delicious dinner at this charming restaurant in Old Lille.

This 7-day itinerary offers a balanced mix of cultural exploration, historical insights, natural beauty, and relaxation, allowing you to experience the best of Lille and its surroundings.

Enjoy your stay!!!!

Printed in Great Britain
by Amazon